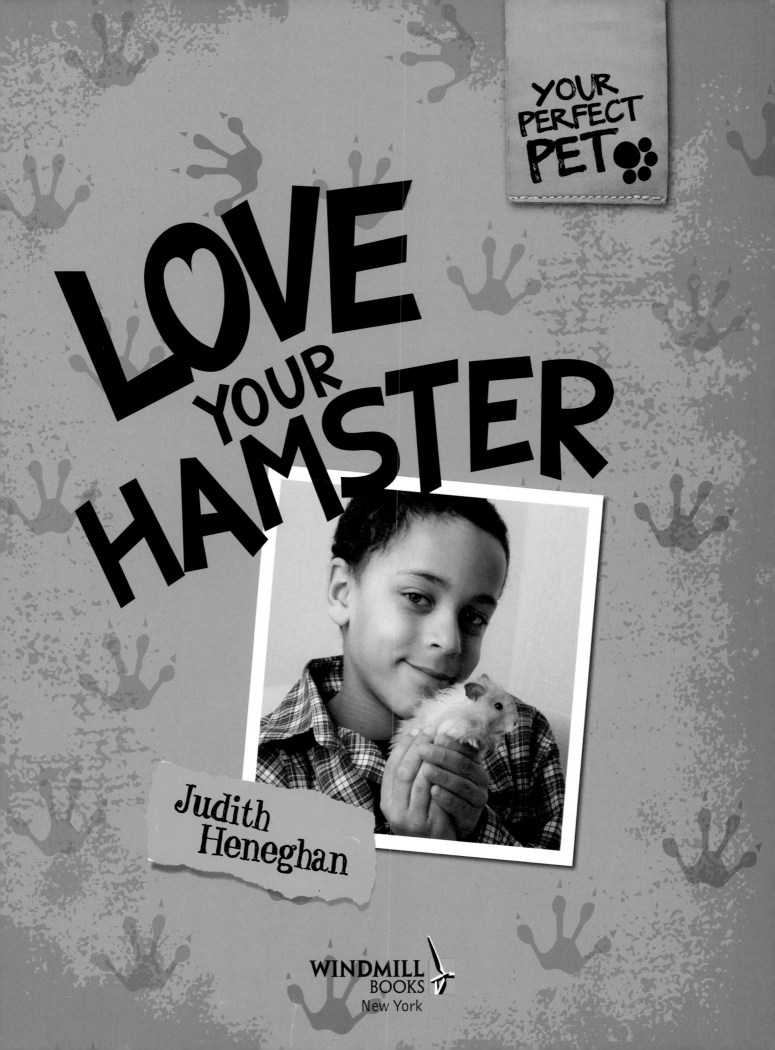

YOUR PERFECT PET

LOVE YOUR HAMSTER

Judith Heneghan

WINDMILL BOOKS
New York

Published in 2013 by Windmill Books, An Imprint of Rosen Publishing
29 East 21st Street, New York, NY 10010

Editor: Nicola Edwards
Designer: Rocket Design (East Anglia) Ltd
Picture Researcher: Nicola Edwards
Consultant: Anna Claxton

Picture Acknowledgements: The author and publisher would like to thank the following for
allowing their pictures to be reproduced in this publication:
Cover (main) Shutterstock © cath5, (inset) © Masterfile/ Janet Bailey; title page © Masterfile/
Janet Bailey; p4 RSPCA Angela Hampton; p5 (t) Shutterstock © Dmitry Naumov, (b)
Shutterstock © Allocricetulus; p6 Shutterstock © AlexKalashnikov; p7(t) Getty Images/
Frederick Florin, (b) Shutterstock © Alexruss; p8 RSPCA Andrew Forsyth/RSPCA; p9(t) ©
Papilio/Alamy, (b) RSPCA Jonathan Plant; p10 cover inset pic; p11(t) © Maximilian Weinzierl/
Alamy, (b) RSPCA Angela Hampton; p12 Shutterstock © Ingrid Prats; p13 (t) Shutterstock ©
cath5, (b) Shutterstock © Sergii Pryshchepa; p14 RSPCA Angela Hampton; p15 (l) Shutterstock
6544696 Carmen Steiner, (r) Shutterstock © AlexandreNunes; p16 (t) Shutterstock © Hintau
Aliaksei, (b) Shutterstock © trgowanlock; p17; RSPCA Chris Brignell; p18 (t) © Alamy Top-Pet-
Pics; p19 RSPCA Chris Brignell; p20 © Alamy Angel Hampton; p21 Shutterstock © Sergieiev;
p22 (t) Shutterstock © Kasiap, (b) Shutterstock © AlexKalashnikov; p23 Shutterstock © Hintau
Aliaksei; p24 © Alamy/tbkmedia.de; p25(t) RSPCA Tim Sambrook, (b) Shutterstock © Zurijeta;
p26 Shutterstock © Rusian Kudrin; p27 (t) RSPCA 1087489 Chris Brignell, (b) Shutterstock
© Alex Bukharov; p28 (t) Shutterstock © MBWTE Photos, (b) Shutterstock © Viachaslau
Kraskouski); p29 © Alamy/imagebroker

Library of Congress Cataloging-in-Publication Data

Heneghan, Judith.
Love your hamster / by Judith Heneghan.
    p. cm. — (Your perfect pet)
Includes index.
ISBN 978-1-4777-0186-7 (library binding) — ISBN 978-1-4777-0200-0 (pbk.) —
ISBN 978-1-4777-0201-7 (6-pack)
1. Hamsters as pets—Juvenile literature. I. Title.
SF459.H3H355 2013
636.935'6—dc23

2012026641

Manufactured in the United States of America

CPSIA Compliance Information: Batch # BW13WM: For Further Information contact Windmill Books, New York, New York at 1-866-478-0556

Contents

My Pet Hamster

My pet hamster's name is Huggles. He's a golden hamster, and he's nearly two years old. He lives in a big cage in my bedroom. His eyes are black, his fur is soft, and his whiskers are tickly. He's a very handsome hamster!

Pet hamsters need to live indoors.

The big question...

Can I have more than one hamster?

Golden hamsters need to live alone. They will fight if put with another hamster. Dwarf hamsters are happy to live in pairs, just as long as they are introduced when they are very young. Make sure you get two males or two females though. One of each will mean lots of babies and you will have to find homes for them all.

Golden hamsters are sometimes called Syrian hamsters. They are the most popular breed. Dwarf hamsters are smaller and faster than golden hamsters. All hamsters need a warm, safe home, a good diet, exercise, toys, and company. This book will help you decide whether a hamster is right for you.

These dwarf hamsters are sisters. They curl up together to keep cozy.

Pet power

In the wild, hamsters live alone. They are territorial, which means they keep to their own area and will fight other hamsters that come too close or try to steal their food.

A Place to Live

We chose a cage for Huggles before we brought him home. The pet store had some colorful little cages, but hamsters like running so I knew he needed a big one. It has a solid plastic floor which makes it easy to clean, and the top half is made of narrow wire bars that Huggles likes to climb. It has two levels so there's plenty to explore.

The big question...

Where should I put my hamster's cage? The best place for your hamster's cage is a warm, quiet corner, away from drafts, direct sunlight, and other pets. If you choose the living room or kitchen, make sure they aren't next to loud appliances. Hamsters are very sensitive to high-pitched sounds.

Hamsters are experts at squeezing through small spaces. The bars on your hamster's cage need to be close together so that it can't escape through the gaps. The door needs to be secured with a strong latch or a lock.

Hamsters have a strong grip. They are excellent climbers.

Furry facts

Hamsters in the wild live in dry deserts or fields. They make their home, or burrow, by tunneling underground. A burrow is safer, warmer, and darker than a home above ground.

Bedding and Nesting

The bottom of Huggles' cage is covered with dust-free wood shavings that we buy from the pet store. I use these as bedding and it helps to keep him clean and dry. Huggles loves to hide bits of food underneath the bedding. Sometimes he piles lots of shavings into the corner of his cage and burrows right into them.

The big question...

What sort of material is best for nesting?

Hay or finely shredded paper such as plain toilet paper is ideal material for a nest. Don't use cotton wool as hamsters can choke on the tiny fibers. Avoid newspaper too, as the ink may be poisonous for your pet.

If you buy a plastic tunnel for your hamster's cage, make sure it is big enough for your hamster to pass through without getting stuck.

Your hamster needs somewhere warm and dark to hide or curl up and sleep. In the wild, hamsters build a nest deep inside their burrow and line it with dried grass and fur. They can't do this in a cage so you will need to help them. Make sure your hamster has a lidded shelter or "nest" with an entrance hole and some nesting material.

This hamster has plenty of cozy bedding to help it sleep comfortably.

Burrowing keeps your hamster interested in its surroundings. It's also good exercise!

Pet power

Hamsters need to dig. They have small, broad feet, with sharp nails that help them burrow underground. Check that the layer of bedding on the floor of the cage is deep enough for your hamster to carry out this natural behavior.

Night and Day

Huggles sleeps at different times than I do. He dozes all day! Luckily he wakes up not long after I get home from school. That's when I play with him. But when I'm ready for bed, he's still awake and active. Sometimes at night I can hear him running around his cage.

The big question...

Can I play with my hamster in the day?

When hamsters are asleep they should be left in peace to get the rest they need. Sometimes hamsters do wake up in the day, but they should never be woken on purpose. The best time to play with your hamster is just before bedtime.

Hamsters are largely nocturnal, which means they sleep in the day and wake up in the early evening. This makes them ideal pets for people who are out at school or work during the day. However, you may prefer to keep the cage out of your bedroom if you are a light sleeper!

Put your hamster's cage in a room where the lights are turned off at around the same time every night.

Pet power

Hamsters don't have good eyesight, but they have great hearing and an excellent sense of smell. Their hearing warns them about approaching danger in the dark, while their sense of smell helps them find food.

A hamster's sensitive whiskers help it find its way in the dark.

Running and Exploring

Huggles sleeps a lot, but when he's awake he's very lively. He races around his cage, jumps off his ladder, and runs along the top of his log tunnel. He also has a special exercise wheel and sometimes he makes it spin so fast that he does a loop-the-loop!

Make sure your hamster's wheel has a solid non-slip surface for running on to stop it from hurting or trapping your hamster's legs.

The big question...

Why do hamsters like running?

Running is a natural instinct for hamsters. In the wild, they need to find food quickly and escape from predators. Exercise wheels allow them to run safely. However, exercise balls can be scary for hamsters. If your hamster exercises outside its cage, watch it carefully to make sure it doesn't get lost.

Hamsters love exploring their surroundings. To stop your hamster from getting bored, place items such as paper towel rolls or small cardboard boxes in its cage.

You could try hiding pieces of food for your hamster to sniff out and discover.

Furry facts

Hamsters have short legs, yet they can run up to 5 miles (8 km) each night!

Let your hamster explore you! Daily handling is great exercise.

Food and Water

Huggles eats special hamster food that we buy from the pet store. I give him one spoonful in a flat dish twice a day. If he doesn't eat it all, I throw the old food out and replace it with a fresh serving. Stale food isn't good for him.

Raw vegetables make healthy treats, but keep portions small. Too much can cause diarrhea.

The big question...

Can I give my hamster other foods? Your hamster may enjoy fresh, crunchy green vegetables, but avoid treats that contain too much fat or sugar. Never give your hamster certain foods such as grapes, oranges, apple seeds, rhubarb, or chocolate as these are poisonous and will make your hamster very sick. If you aren't sure, ask your vet's advice.

Hamsters, like all small animals, need a constant supply of fresh water. The best way to give this to them is through a metal-spouted water bottle which can be hung from the bars of their cage. Water in a bowl is easily spilled or soiled. Remember to change the water every day!

Make sure your hamster's water bottle has a metal spout like this one that your hamster can't chew!

Pet power

Hamsters are rodents, which means they belong to a group of animals including mice, rats, and squirrels with strong front teeth that are perfect for opening tough nut shells and seed cases. They love to gnaw on anything hard, such as wooden blocks.

Stuffed Cheeks

Huggles never eats all of his food at once. He stuffs some of it into special pouches inside his cheeks and saves it for later. I can always tell when his pouches are full. His head looks twice its usual size!

Pet power

Hamsters store food in their pouches because in the wild it is too dangerous to stop and eat it out in the open. A predator such as an owl may attack them, or they may have to fight another hamster that has found the same food source.

Hamsters can store up to half their body weight in their pouches.

In the wild, hamsters spend most of their waking hours searching or foraging for a range of foods including seeds, berries, and some small insects. When they find food, they either stuff it in their pouches to take back to their nest or hide it in secret places along the way. A hamster may have several different stores of food in its burrow or cage.

Furry facts

Hamsters have five toes on their front feet, but only three toes on their back feet. They use their front feet like hands to grip food.

Holding Your Hamster

When Huggles first arrived I didn't handle him very much. I just talked to him and let him sniff my hand. It took him a couple of weeks to get used to me. Now he doesn't mind being picked up. He comes and sits on my hand if I put it flat on the floor of his cage.

First let your hamster get used to your smell.

The big question...

Will my hamster bite me?
Young hamsters sometimes bite if they are startled. If this happens, simply put your hamster back in its cage but don't stop handling it. Be careful not to scare your hamster and be patient.

18

Once your hamster knows your voice and your smell, it is a good idea to hold it every day. Try stroking it, then picking it up for a short while. The best position for holding your hamster is while you are sitting on the floor. Then, if your hamster wriggles out of your hands, it is less likely to hurt itself.

Dwarf hamsters can be more difficult to hold safely as they move quickly. Always keep your hamster between two open cupped hands.

Pet power

Hamsters are always on the lookout for predators such as owls that might swoop down from the sky and grab them. So when you pick up your hamster, don't lower your hand over it and try to grab it. Your hamster will run away!

Always scoop up your hamster from underneath, letting it sniff your hands first.

Keeping Clean

I like cleaning out Huggles' cage. First I scoop out all the old wood shavings and put them in the garbage. Then I wipe the floor, the nesting box, and the exercise wheel with a damp cloth. When it is dry I put in plenty of new bedding and nesting material.

Don't forget to wash your hands after cleaning out the cage.

The big question...

How often should I clean out the cage?

The bedding and nesting materials need changing once a week. However, getting rid of all the familiar scent markings can be stressful for your hamster, so always leave a little of the old material in the nest. This way, your hamster will still feel at home.

Hamsters like to keep clean and regularly wash by licking themselves. However, their cages become dirty where they go to the bathroom, and some areas become full of leftover food and seed husks. Your hamster's cage needs to be cleaned to stop your hamster from picking up diseases and infections.

Furry facts

All hamsters have scent glands. These small, raised lumps look a little like freckles or moles. Golden hamsters have one on each hip, while dwarf hamsters have them underneath, around their tail areas. They rub them against objects to mark them with their own distinctive smell.

Hamsters wash and spread their scent at the same time.

Going Away

Last year we went on vacation so I asked my friend Dan to look after Huggles. We took Huggles in his cage to Dan's house, along with a supply of food. Huggles doesn't know Dan very well, so I asked Dan not to pick him up unless Huggles came to him and sat on his hand.

The big question...

What if I am going away for just one night?

If you and your family are going away for just one night, it is probably kinder to leave your hamster at home alone, as a move can be quite stressful. Ask someone to come in and check that your hamster is secure and that it has enough water and food.

Always find someone to care for your hamster if you need to go away. Make sure this person has plenty of time to look after your pet, and give them a checklist so that they remember what to do. If they have other pets such as cats or dogs, ask them to keep your hamster in a separate room.

Pet power

Hamsters find sudden change stressful. Don't take them to different locations unless you have to. Transport them in a familiar cage with a breathable cover such as a towel over the top. The darkness will help them stay calm when they are traveling.

Never transport your hamster in a cardboard box as it will quickly gnaw its way out and escape.

Staying Healthy

I take a good look at Huggles every day. I watch for any changes that may mean he's not feeling well. He's a very healthy hamster most of the time, but once I noticed a lump above his eye. We took him to the vet who said he had an infection and gave him some medicine. The lump soon went away.

Long-haired hamsters need regular grooming with a soft brush to keep their fur clean and healthy.

The big question...

What is wet tail?
Wet tail is a very dangerous illness for hamsters. It is a little like diarrhea. If you notice any staining or soiling around your hamster's bottom, take it to the vet right away.

Because hamsters are prey animals, they hide any signs of illness for as long as possible to avoid being attacked by predators. So if you do notice any changes in your hamster such as new lumps, sticky eyes, a dirty bottom, or not drinking and eating then don't wait. Speak to your vet.

This hamster is being examined by a vet.

Furry facts

Hamsters can catch colds from humans. A cold will make your hamster feel very unwell. If you have a cold yourself, ask someone else to look after your hamster until you are feeling better.

Getting Older

Huggles is nearly two now. That's quite old for a hamster. He's not as fast as he used to be, but the vet says this is normal for a hamster of his age. He's still bright-eyed and lively!

If you have two dwarf hamsters and don't want hamster babies, make sure you have two males or two females.

The big question...

My hamster's teeth seem far too long. What should I do?

A hamster with overgrown teeth will find it difficult and painful to eat. You should take your hamster to the vet, as it may need an operation to have its teeth trimmed.

As your hamster gets older, you may find it slows down a little. As well as the usual health checks, make sure its teeth and nails are not getting too long. Your hamster may enjoy gnawing on a wooden chew block. A bowl of sand makes a great place to dig and helps keep your hamster's nails trimmed.

Most hamsters live between two and three years, though dwarf hamsters often have shorter lives.

Furry facts

Hamsters are rodents, which means their front teeth never stop growing. In the wild the tips are constantly worn down by chewing and gnawing on hard seeds and nuts.

Best Friends

Huggles is a fantastic pet and we have loads of fun. Today I watched him burying some food in the corner behind his exercise wheel. Then he covered it with some paper from his nest. He may be soft and cuddly, but he's smart, too! I love caring for him.

Pet power

Pet hamsters are fascinating animals that still display many of the characteristics of their relatives in the wild. Does your hamster ever stand up on its hind legs, very still, eyes alert? Hamsters are sensitive to danger, and they constantly pick up signals from the world outside their cage.

Hamsters are always alert to possible danger.

Hamsters make great pets because they enjoy human attention, have lively, quirky personalities, and don't take up too much space at home. They are also cheaper to care for than some types of pet, though you'll need to buy regular supplies of food and bedding and vet bills can be expensive.

Furry facts

Hamsters can learn to come when they hear their name. Try putting your hand in the cage with a small treat and say your hamster's name. When it comes, let it have the reward. It will soon get the message!

With plenty of care and attention, hamsters make wonderful pets.

Quiz

How well do you know hamsters? Try this quick quiz to find out!

1. Imagine you are a hamster and you've just found a nice fat sunflower seed on the ground. Do you:
   a. stuff it in your pouch and run to the safety of your nest before any other animals see you?
   b. squeak to let all the other hamsters in the area know you've found some food?
   c. leave it because you can always come back for it later?

2. Next you see a large black shape in the sky above your head. Do you think it is:
   a. a friendly human?
   b. a cloud?
   c. an owl searching for prey to eat?

3. When you notice this black shape, do you:
   a. ignore it—it won't see you?
   b. jump up and down to frighten it off?
   c. run and hide?

4. You're hungry, but it's pitch black and your eyesight isn't very good. Do you:
   a. wait until the sun comes up so you can see where you're going?
   b. use your nose to sniff out food, and use your whiskers to detect obstacles in the dark?
   c. feel your way forward with your paws?

5. You're not feeling very well. Do you:
   a. try to hide your illness because looking sick in the open exposes you to predators?
   b. squeak to get a human to take you to the vet?
   c. eat a few extra berries because they're good for you?

6. You are in a small cardboard box which is moving around all over the place. Do you:
   a. sit back and enjoy the ride?
   b. gnaw a hole in the box and get out of there as fast as you can?
   c. eat a few seeds you've stored in your pouches?

Glossary

balanced diet (BAL-ensd DY-ut) A healthy variety of food.

bedding material (BEH-ding muh-TEER-ee-ul) Material such as wood shavings that cover the cage floor.

burrow (BUR-oh) A nest in an underground tunnel.

desert (DEH-zurt) Dry, hot part of the world.

diarrhea (dy-uh-REE-uh) Having very watery stools and having to go very often.

foraging (FOR-ij-ing) Searching for food such as seeds and berries.

gnaw (NAW) To use front teeth to cut and bite.

grooming (GROOM-ing) Keeping fur clean.

nesting material (NEST-ing muh-TEER-ee-ul) Hay or shredded paper for lining a shelter or burrow to keep warm.

nocturnal (nok-TUR-nul) Awake at night.

pouches (POWCH-es) Pockets inside a hamster's cheeks.

predators (PREH-duh-terz) Animals that hunt for food.

prey (PRAY) An animal that is hunted for food.

rodents (ROH-dents) Small animals such as hamsters, mice, and rats that use their front teeth to gnaw through their food.

scent glands (SENT GLANDZ) Parts of the body that produce a special scent for marking territory.

territorial (ter-uh-TAWR-ee-ul) Keeping to one area.

wet tail (WET TAYL) A disease with symptoms of diarrhea.

Index

Websites

For web resources related to the subject of this book, go to:
www.windmillbooks.com/weblinks
and select this book's title.